High Profit, Low Risk Trading Methods

How to Make Money and Protect Assets in Today's Financial Markets

by
George H. Kariger

ISBN-13: 978-1492208990
ISBN-10: 149220899X

For

My Wonderful Family

Table of Contents

Introduction

"Life isn't meant to be ordinary, but extraordinary."
-Anonymous

An amazing event occurred in a fifth grade classroom in a small school in a little town in northern Indiana in the spring of 2001. Four ten and eleven year old year children figured out how to master the stock market and make over $36,000 on a $100,000 investment in only ten weeks in the United States stock market. During these weeks the stock market declined over 25%.

These children participated in the Indiana Economic Council's spring stock market simulation. They defeated over 2000 other teams in Indiana, including high school teams guided by business and economic teachers.

During this time period they soundly trounced the investment performances of most professional stock market managers on Wall Street.

The secret to their success was that their small team closely examined stock charts of U.S. Companies and invested their money with the *trend of the strongest moving stocks*. Another team in the same classroom used essentially the same strategies and led the state contest most of the ten weeks.

Where are these children from one of the smallest school systems in the state now? In junior high Randy moved six miles north to a bigger school and was the top player on the Indiana state basketball champions in 2007. Considered one of the top players in the state, he played on the Indiana All-Stars and was the point guard and floor leader of NCAA Division I Ball State University. Steve, an outstanding academic student and also an excellent high school basketball player, went to Purdue University and traveled the country with the outstanding Purdue Varsity Glee Club. He is currently a chemical engineering intern for Archer Daniels Midland Company and is a production engineer at Cargill. Maegan, a daughter of the town's Baptist pastor, stayed in that small town and is a superb person and mother. Kristen, a wonderful young lady, attended Ivy Tech College and is working at the Zimmer Corporation.

I had the honor of being the teacher of these children and teaching at this little school corporation for thirty-five years. I have many former students who have become outstanding doctors, nurses, lawyers, teachers, missionaries, pastors, soldiers, engineers, business men and women, and even a successful major league baseball starting pitcher. I like to think I had a part in their success, but I think the credit goes to their parents and the values of the small community and their small school where they attended.

For many years my students participated in the Indiana Stock Market Simulation and a fair amount of times finished in the top ten among hundreds of teams in the state.

I have been an investor and trader for over 25 years, studied stock market trading systems intensively, and read hundreds of books on the topic. I feel that simple systems are often the best, and that's why I decided to write this book. You simply don't need complicated systems and charts full of indicators to make good timing decisions in the financial markets. All that will do that is confuse you and make it more difficult for you to make the right decisions.

Hopefully this information will help the investor to not only grow his investments, but to help protect him from losses during bear markets. No one enjoys opening up their monthly and quarterly retirement account statements and seeing large percentage drops. This book is designed to give you simple methods which will help you time the markets, so that you can both safely grow and protect your money at the same time.

Chapter 1
What It Takes to Win

"We must become the change we want to see."
Mahatma Gandhi

There are a number of steps to earning profits and reducing risks in the financial markets. I have been a trader and investor since 1985. I've spent thousands of hours studying hundreds of trading and investing books and articles and have tried many methods.

To be successful you must have a system which does the following:

1. Captures most of the gains in the big up trends;
2. Protects against losing a large portion of your assets in the large downtrends;
3. Diversifies among the main asset categories of stocks bonds, real estate, commodities, and currencies.

Surviving to invest and trade another day are of the highest importance. You can lose 50% or more of your money when you hold your investments during difficult markets such as the bear stock markets which occurred in the United States during the 1930's, 1973-1974, 2001-2002, and 2008.

The conventional advice to buy and hold

becomes buy and hope. Most people do not have the emotional tolerance to lose large percentages of their investments and then wait for their investments to recover.

If you capture the majority of the gains in large up trends, then you can sometimes double or triple the value of your investments within a decade or less.

Diversification of investments among stocks, bonds, real estate, commodities, currencies, and money market funds help ensure against large swings in your overall portfolio and reduce risk. Although in severe bear markets and crashes, stocks, real estate, and commodities often experience sharp declines together, bonds, currencies, and money market funds can often help provide some protection during such times.

Chapter 2
Choose a Time Frame

"Order and simplification are the first steps toward mastery of a subject."
-Thomas Mann

One of the first decisions you need to make is choosing your trading time frame. Are you a short term trader, an intermediate term trader, or a long term investor?

Short term traders use 15, 30, or 60 minute stock charts. If you want to trade using 5 or 10 minute charts, you will be glued to your trading charts and computer most of the trading day. You will make numerous trades and your trading costs of commissions and bid-ask spreads will be higher. Your risk will be lower, because ideally you will be out of your trades before any of them incur large losses.

Intermediate term traders will use daily and weekly charts. Positions will be held for weeks to months. Trading costs will be lower, but risks may be higher due to larger holding times. If you're an intermediate term trader, you may need to look at your charts once a day or maybe only once a week. Risks will be higher, because you will be holding your investments for a longer time period and there will be more ups and downs in your security holdings. However, risk can be mitigated by using methods which will be described later in this book.

Long term investors will use weekly and monthly charts. It's important to remember that a long term investor should not become a long term buy and holder. The stock market meltdown of 2008 caused some investors to lose over 50% of their assets over just a period of several months. Tech investors lost a high percentages of their assets in the technology stock crash of 2001-2002. The technology-heavy NASDAQ Composite Index never recovered to the highs that were made in 1999. It took decades for stock market indexes to recover from the stock market meltdowns that occurred during the Great Depression years of the 1930's.

A long term investor will be exposed to greater risks due to the ups and downs of the financial markets, but trading expenses will be lower. Potential rewards for long term investors can be high, but no one should become a long term buy and holder. The experiences of Enron and some technology stocks which lost 90% or more of their value during the last decade should teach all of us that the conventional philosophy of buy, hold, and never sell any stock or financial market is very risky.

For many the intermediate term time frame is a good compromise between short term and long term trading.   There is a better way of investing and trading which is available to all. Using a few simple timing tools, traders and investors can beat buy and hold. There are ways to earn higher returns with less risk. This book will show you how to do exactly that.

Chapter 3
Determine the Trend

"In investment management, the real opportunity to achieve superior results is not in scrambling to outperform the market, but in establishing and adhering to appropriate investment policies over the long term – policies that position the portfolio to benefit from riding with the main long-term forces in the market."
-Charles Ellis, Investment Policy

After you have chosen your time frame, the first step you will need to take is to determine the overall trend of the financial market you are analyzing. There are many methods of determining the trend. The market has only three directions it can be trending - up, down, or sideways.

Your primary trend identification method is making sure that you *always* trade with the trend. It is much easier to trade in the direction of the longer term trend rather than trying to make money by scalping profits in counter trend trading. "The trend is your friend" is not only a popular saying, but is also very true.

You can identify an uptrend by any of these methods:

1. The current price of your selected market index or ETF is above the **rising** 50 day

exponential moving average (EMA). If the price is above is above the **falling** 50 day exponential moving average, then there is a good chance that the price will fall and decline below the 50 day EMA. A declining 50 day EMA often serves as a ceiling to prices.

2. The current price is above the 200 day simple moving average (SMA) or the 10 month exponential moving average (EMA).

3. If the 50 day EMA is above the 200 day SMA, the market is considered to be in an uptrend. Likewise, when the 50 day EMA is below the 200 day SMA, then a downtrend is indicated.

4. An EMA crossover method could be utilized. As an example, if the 10 day EMA is located above the 50 day EMA, then the market trend is considered to be in an uptrend and to be in a downtrend if the opposite occurs.

Markets often move sideways or are stuck in ranges, with no uptrend nor downtrend. These are indicated by flat 50 day moving averages that are neither up-sloping nor down-sloping, numerous crosses of the price above and below the 50 or 200 day moving averages within several weeks, or markets that exhibit a lot of volatility up and down with sharp increases and sharp decreases in price within a few weeks. When you place several moving averages on a chart, such as the 10, 20 and 50 day EMA's, the averages will be constantly crossing over each other and will often be very close to each other. All of these are indications that the market is going sideways.

Stay out of sideways markets. You make money in trending markets. If you participate in sideways markets, you will experience many whipsaws. You will be buying when the market goes up a little and selling when the market goes down a little. It's a way for your assets to get eaten up by trading commissions and small losses.

Sometimes market prices will go back and forth around their 50 or 200 day moving averages, leading to trading whipsaws. This is because the 50 and 200 day moving average are the most heavily followed moving average in the financial markets, and sometimes markets become indecisive at these points. One way to handle this problem is to only buy if the market price goes a certain percentage above the 200 day moving averarge, such as 1%-4% above the 50 day or 200 day MA. Vice versa, some traders only sell once the price goes 1%-4% below the 50 or 200 day MA. This helps reduce the number of whipsaws.

When prices are below their 50 day EMA or 200 day SMA, and the moving averages are sloping down, it indicates that the direction of the market is down. It is a time to stay out of the market. You could short these markets or purchase inverse ETF's. Inverse ETF's make money when market prices are falling. ProShares are one of the leading providers of inverse ETF's in the United States.

I do not prefer shorting markets or purchasing inverse ETF's. It is more difficult to make money by shorting stocks or markets which are decreasing in price. Market prices usually move more quickly in bear markets and are more volatile. Prices often drop quickly and sharply in a bear market, but there are also days in bear markets when the counter-trend moves up can be sharp. There is a much greater chance of error when a trader participates in bear markets because of the speed that markets move.

Why do prices fall more quickly in bear markets than the speed that prices increase in bull markets? It's because fear is a stronger emotion than greed in human beings. When a bear market ensues, a lot of traders run for the exit quickly out of fear.

Once again, we are looking to buy markets and ETF's with increasing prices and up sloping moving averages. That's when we make our money.

If a longer term trading method appeals to you, you could use a weekly rather than a daily system to determine the overall trend. For instance, an uptrend on the weekly charts exists when all of the following are true:

1. RSI (14) on the weekly charts is above 50; and
2. Using MACD (12,26,9), the MACD is above its slow line, and
3. Using Slow Stochastics (14,3), the fast line is above the slow line.

The main thing to remember is that we only buy markets or ETF's when the overall trend is up.

In the next several pages we will examine charts to examine the overall trend on them.

The uptrend for the Dow Jones Industrial Average began when the price crossed the 50 day EMA and 200 day SMA at the beginning of 2013. The 50 day EMA is above the 200 day SMA and the 50 day EMA is increasing nicely at the start of 2013, all indicating an up trending market.

From March thru June the Bullish US Dollar ETF is in an uptrend, using the 50 and 200 day EMA's as a guide. From June through August UUP becomes difficult to trade, going mostly sideways with large up and down price spikes.

SPY S&P 500 SPDRs NYSE
31-Dec-2008 O 81.03 H 82.75 L 80.84 C 82.08 V 213.4M Chg +1.16 (+1.43%) ▲
♦ SPY (Daily) 82.08
━EMA(50) 82.92
━MA(200) 106.35

In the latter half of 2008 the SPY ETF price is below the decreasing 50 day EMA, which is below the 200 day SMA. This is a dangerous bear market. The decreasing 50 day EMA is serving as a ceiling to prices.

GLD SPDR Gold Trust Shares NYSE
31-Jul-2013   Close 127.96 Volume 16.0M Chg -0.16 (-0.12%) ▾
GLD (Daily) 127.96
EMA(50) 128.95 170.01
MA(200) 149.63

164.40
162.30
158.39
150.84
143.43
137.62
130.14
130.51   130.85
127.96
114.68

Sep Oct Nov Dec 2013 Feb Mar Apr May Jun Jul

MACD(19,39,9) -1.122, -1.988, 0.866
0.866
0
-1.122
-1.988

Sep Oct Nov Dec 2013 Feb Mar Apr May Jun Jul

From mid-October thru December of 2012 the chart of gold prices shows sideways movement – moving averages are going sideways. At the start of 2013 the down sloping 50 day EMA begins to show a declining market. In Feb. the bear market is confirmed with the 50 day EMA crossing below the 200 day simple moving average.

This weekly chart of TLT, the 20+ year treasury bond ETF shows a bull market beginning during the month of April 2012 with the RSI rising above 50, the fast line crossing above the slow line in the Slow Stochastic, and the MACD line crossing above its slow line shortly thereafter. In May of 2013 the RSI, the Slow Stochastic, and the MACD indicate the bear market in TLT is beginning.

This weekly chart of the commodities DBC ETF indicates a strong bull market from January thru June, 2008. In July 2008 DBC begins a downtrend shown by RSI closing below 50, a MACD line crossing its slow line, and the Slow Stochastic fast line crossing below its slow line. The market continues to decline thru the rest of the fall 2008.

Chapter 4

Timing Your Entry

"Buy some good stock and hold it till it goes up, then sell it. If it don't go up, don't buy it."

-Will Rogers

After you have determined that the overall trend is up, then you time your entry using a momentum indicator. The MACD indicator, found in almost every stock charting website or software, could be used for this purpose. Gerald Appel invented the MACD and in his book *Technical Analysis: Power Tools for Active Investors* described its use:

(1) Rather than using the standard MACD setting of 12-26-9, Appel recommends a faster setting of 6-19-9 for entries. Buy when the MACD line crosses above the slower line;

(2) The True Strength Index (TSI) indicator with the standard 25-13-7 setting could be used in lieu of or as an added confirmation of MACD buys. Buy when the TSI line crosses above its average.

The MACD 6-19-9 can be used to re-enter the market to buy when the overall trend is up.

$INDU Dow Jones Industrial Average INDX
31-May-2013 **Last** 15115.57 **Volume** 744.5M **Chg** -208.96 (-1.36%) ▾
₩ $INDU (Daily) 15115.57   15542.40
—EMA(50) 14892.19
—MA(200) 13816.50

Here are some charts which illustrate good entry points in an overall uptrend. A good buy entry is indicated in mid-November 2012 for the Dow Jones Industrial Average, when the MACD crosses above its slower line. If you are shaken out of a trade and wish to reenter, good buying points also occur in late December, late February 2013, and late April. The reenter point in mid-April was not as timely, but with the overall larger trend up, the trade eventually works well.

The True Strength Index (TSI), found in many stock charting programs, may be used instead of or in conjunction with the MACD.

25

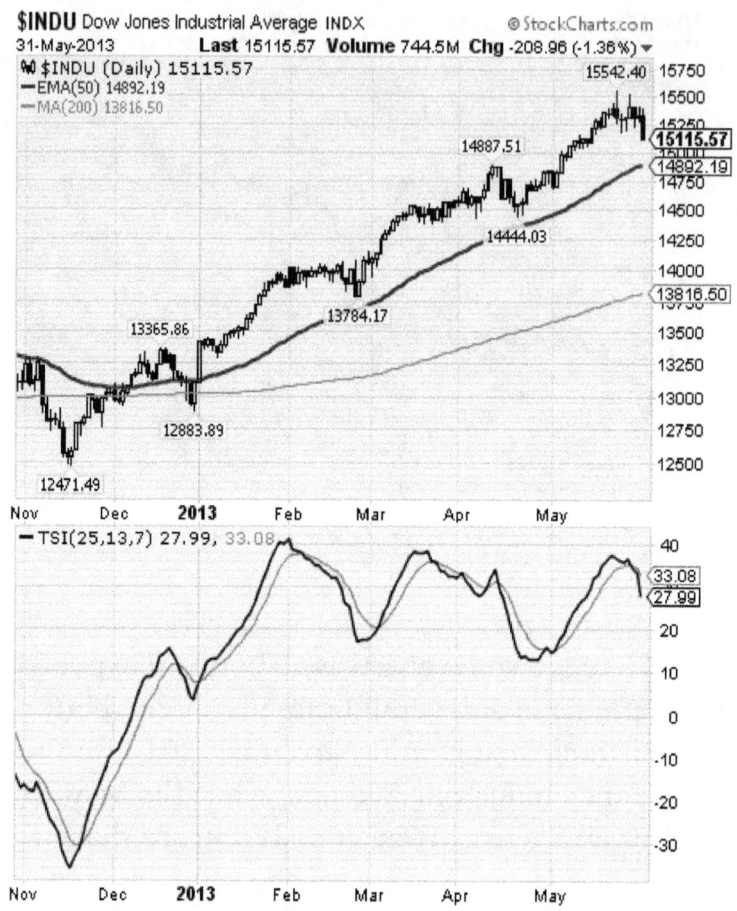

Using the same chart, we can see the overall trend is up, with the 50 day EMA rising and sitting above the 200 day SMA. The TSI is used instead of the MACD, and the timing of the buys is very similar to the previous chart.

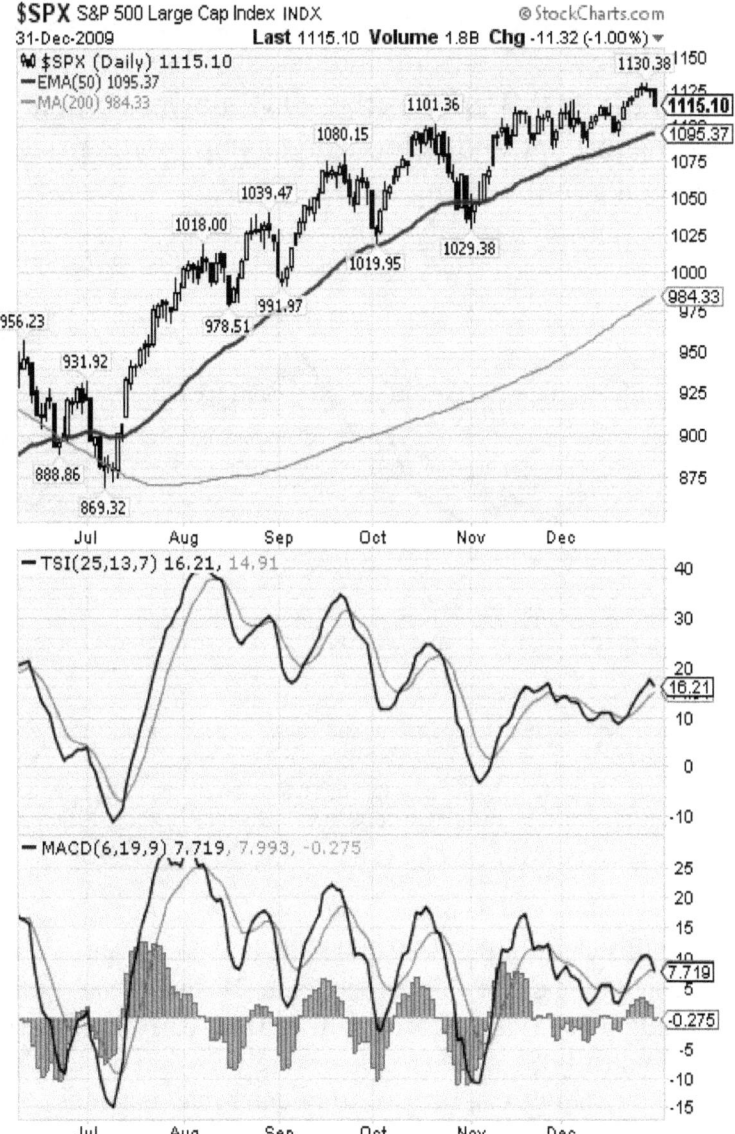

After the crash in late 2008, a major buying point occurs in July 2009 in the S&P 500 index when the 50 day EMA crosses the 200 day SMA and the MACD and TSI crosses occur in early July, indicating buy points.

Another good option to pinpoint buy entries is to use the ADX, a trend indicator. A buy occurs when the +DMI crosses the -DMI upward when the overall uptrend is indicated as up by the price being above the rising 50 day EMA.

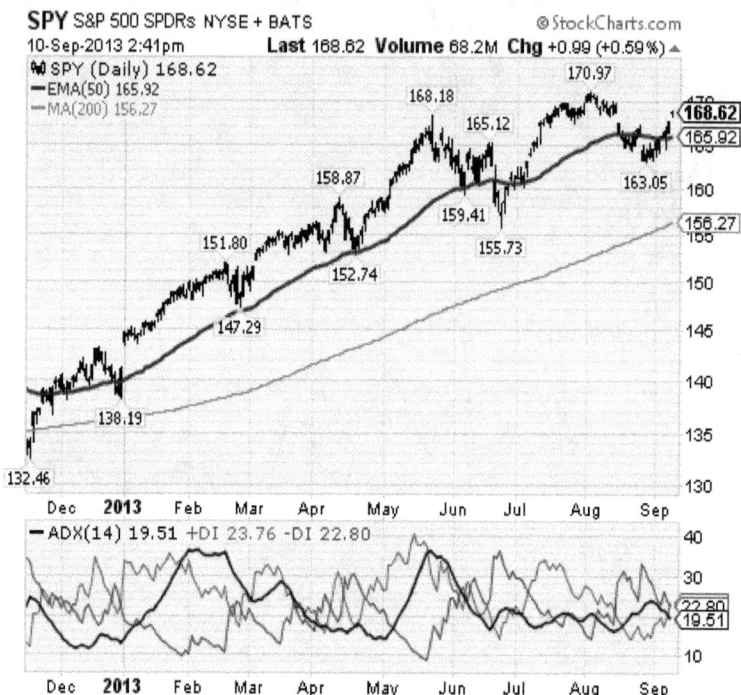

In this chart of the S&P 500 ETF, buy points are indicated by the DI+ line crossing the DI- line at the start of January 2013, late February, mid-April, early June, early July, and early September. Most were very timely signals. These buy points can be used to re-enter markets or as times to make additional investments. Of course, no signal is perfect, which is why using stop losses and trailing stops are important.

When using the ADX indicator, it is more important to use the troughs and peaks of the ADX to time trades rather than to use the values of the indicator. For instance, many times a timely buy occurs when the ADX has bottomed and begins to rise. The main caution when using the indicator to buy is that you absolutely must be sure that the overall trend is up.

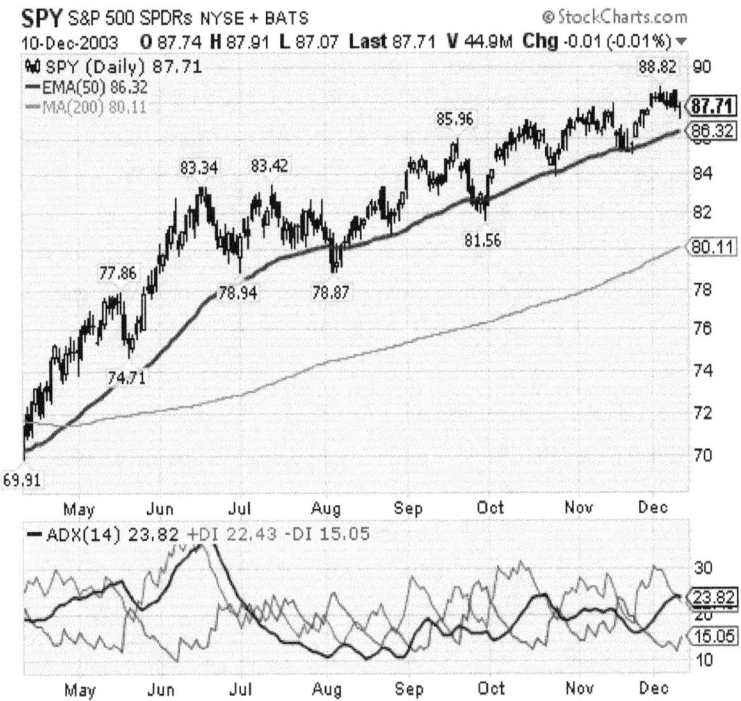

Using the ADX "trough method," the dark black ADX line indicates troughs in May, October, and November, all excellent buying points and re-entry points in the larger overall uptrend. It's good to wait for a few days of confirmation of increasing prices after the ADX has bottomed to avoid possible whipsaws.

Charles D. Kirkpatrick in his book, *Kirkpatrick's Investment and Trading Strategies: Tools and Techniques for Profitable Trend Following* detailed many of these innovative ways to use ADX peaks and troughs, along with other indicators and systems to make good investing and trading decisions. His book is highly recommended.

Chapter 5
Timing Your Exit

"In character, in manner, in style, in all things, the supreme excellence is simplicity."

-Henry Wadsworth Longfellow

After you have made your buy, it's very important to know when the trend is changing. If you try to using moving average crossovers to exit, they often get you out of a trade too slowly. Many times you end up giving up a large amount of the profit you have made or the profit turns into a loss by the time the moving averages cross to the downside.

Using a momentum indicator is a good way to exit a trade. Usually momentum slows before the overall trend changes. Some good methods of exiting trades are:

> (1.)   Gerald Appel in his book *Technical Analysis: Power Tools for Active Investors* recommends using the MACD with the setting of 19-39-9 for trade exits. This is slower than the standard 12-26-9 setting. What often happens with the 12-26-9

setting is that you are shaken out of the trade too soon and then a whipsaw occurs with the market quickly recovering. The sell should occur when the MACD line (19-39-9) crosses below its slower line.

(2.)　　　The True Strength Index (TSI) indicator with the standard 25-13-7 indicator could be used in lieu of or in combination with the 19-39-9 MACD for exits. When the TSI line crosses below its average line, an exit occurs.

(3.)　　　A third possibility is to use the TRIX (Triple Exponential Average) indicator with the setting 15-9. It is another momentum indicator, which will give very similar signals to the MACD or TSI. It is found in many standard charting programs. On page 34 is an example of the S&P 500 daily chart from late 2012 through August of 2013. A rising 50 day EMA is above the 200 day SMA, showing that the market is in an overall uptrend. For the most part the sell signals are given roughly at the same times by the TSI, MACD, and TRIX. The good thing about using momentum indicators for sell signals is that a sell is often given during sideways trending *before* the market begins a steep decline. In most cases using a momentum indicator gets the investor out of the market before sharp declines.

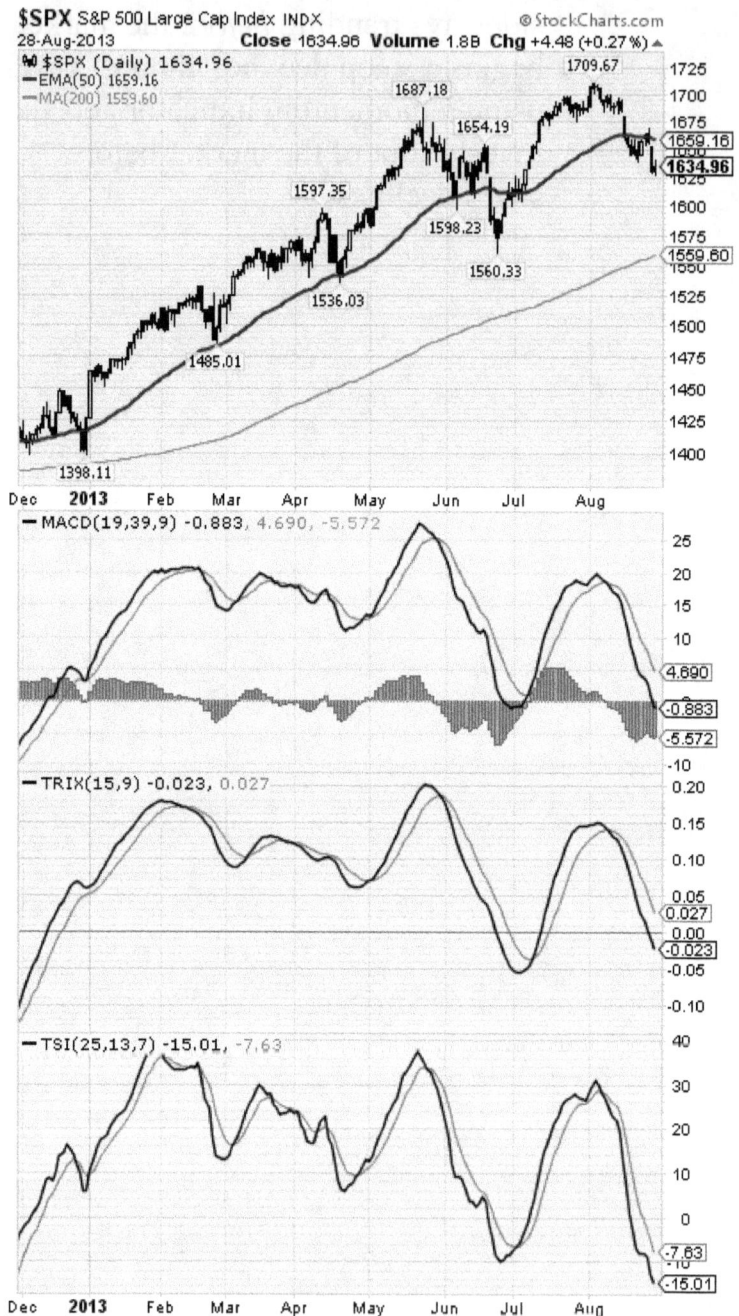

The DBC (Commodities) ETF on the next page shows an uptrend with rising moving averages and the 50 day EMA above the 200 day SMA. A good selling point occurs in mid-July 2008 with the down sloping 50 day EMA and the MACD and TRIX crossovers. Had you waited to sell until late September for the moving average crossover, you would have lost money.

The ADX indicator can also used to accurately time exits. When the ADX peaks and then a downtrend is confirmed by a few days of price action, it is time to exit the market. ADX peaks are heavily correlated with market reversals.

The ADX makes two peaks in September 2000 in this chart of the Dow Jones Industrial Average. In both cases the market follows with sharp downside drops. In late October the ADX peaks, which leads to yet another reversal of the market trend. In this case the market was trending sharply downward, the ADX peaked, and the index reversed and rallied sharply. ADX peaks often indicate reversals in current price direction. The Dow Jones Industrial Average then trended sideways, and the ADX decreased, confirming the lack of direction in the market. Stay out of sideways trending markets. Sideways markets are indicated by sideways moving averages.

The QQQ technology shares ETF shows two distinct ADX peaks on this chart, both which lead to dramatic price reversals. In late September of 2012 ADX peaked warning of a price reversal from the uptrend to a steep downtrend. In November of 2012, ADX again peaked, warning that the odds were in favor of the downtrend reversing into a new uptrend. Both ADX peaks were timely signals. The ADX peak system is not 100% right all the time, as no indicator is always correct. It is always good to wait for a couple of days of confirming price action to act on ADX peaks. Keep stops in place in case the indicator gives an incorrect signal. However, ADX peaks and the MACD 19-39-9 systems are right more often than they are wrong in providing early identification of when to exit the market.

Chapter 6
Avoiding Crashes and Bear Markets

"It ain't what you don't know that gets you into trouble. It's what you know for sure that just ain't so."

-Mark Twain

"Risk comes from not knowing what you're doing."

-Warren Buffett

This is probably the most important chapter in the book. No one wants to lose large amounts of their money to the markets. Most of the time markets give strong hints that they are weakening, giving traders and investors time to exit before the real damage begins.

If you are a conservative investor like me, there are certain times when you absolutely must *not* be in the market. You can use these guidelines whether you are trading in the stock, bond, commodity, precious metals, or currency markets.

You must not be in market when either of the following situations exist:

(1.)   When the 50 day EMA is below the 200 day SMA; This rule alone will keep you out of many destructive bear markets and crashes;

(2.)   Using the MACD 19-39-9 setting, never invest when the MACD line is below 0 *and* the MACD line is below its slow line.

These are simple rules that will help protect your funds from the very large majority of bear markets and crashes. Following these rules would have gotten you out of the stock market **before** the 1929 crash, the 1973-74 bear market, the 1987 crash, the 2001-2002 NASDAQ crash, and the severe bear market of 2008.

Bear markets are usually very volatile, with many large down days and some very big up days, which sometimes trick investors into buying when they should be staying out of the market. Some of the biggest up days in history have been during severe bear markets, but do not be tricked or fooled by them. Continue to follow these simple rules.

Buy and hold, and never selling an investment will also expose you to large losses, some from which you may never recover. It is the advice that some stockbrokers and professionals give their clients, but it is very risky advice. Some stocks never do recover, and some markets are underwater for decades. Buy and hold, and never selling is **not** a conservative investing philosophy. It is **very risky** approach to investing and trading.

In the large majority of cases, a market will

begin to deteriorate for awhile before bear markets begin or markets crash. Large crashes almost never occur when prices are above rising moving averages and the MACD line is above 0.

The following pages will contain examples of markets which you should avoid, using the 2 major sell guidelines which I have detailed. The QQQ (mostly technology stocks) ETF began a steep fall beginning around October 2000. The following chart shows the deep decline from a high of $97.89 to a low of $18.69 two years later. The 50 day EMA crossed below the 200 day SMA in October of 2000, giving warning of an impending decline. During most of the two years the MACD daily line remained below 0, and many of the sharpest declines were when the 19-39-9 MACD was below 0 and the MACD line was below its slow line. In August of 2013, QQQ was priced at $75.15 and has still not recovered to the price it was in the fall of 2000. This is an example of when "buy and hold" became a decade of "buy and hope."

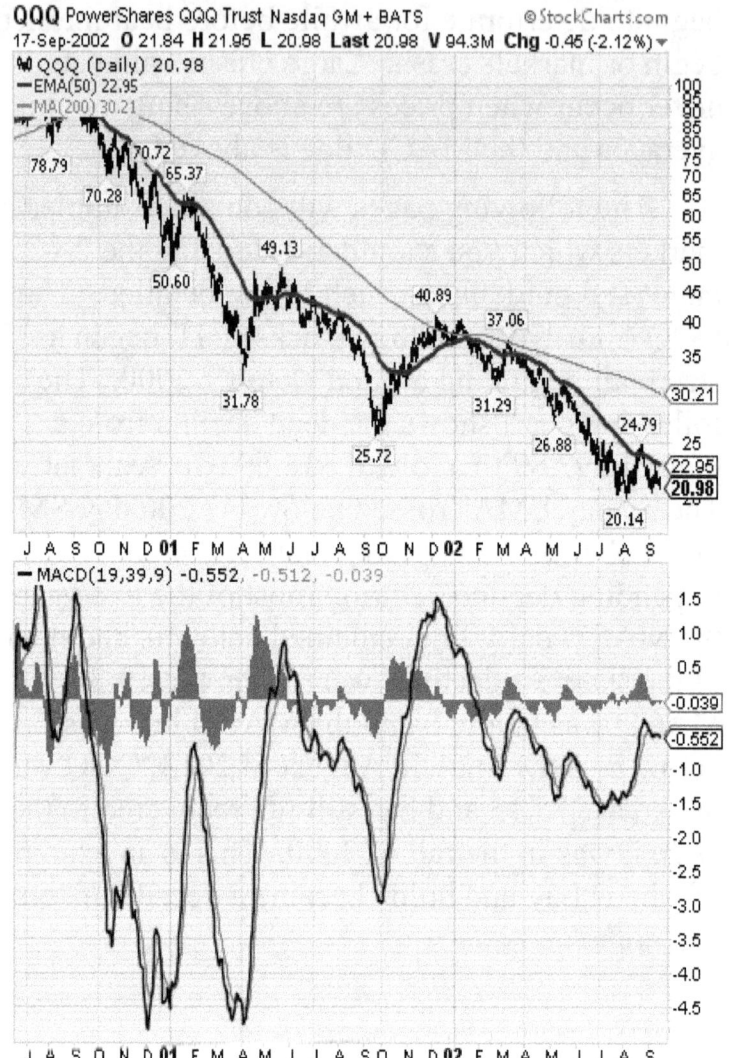

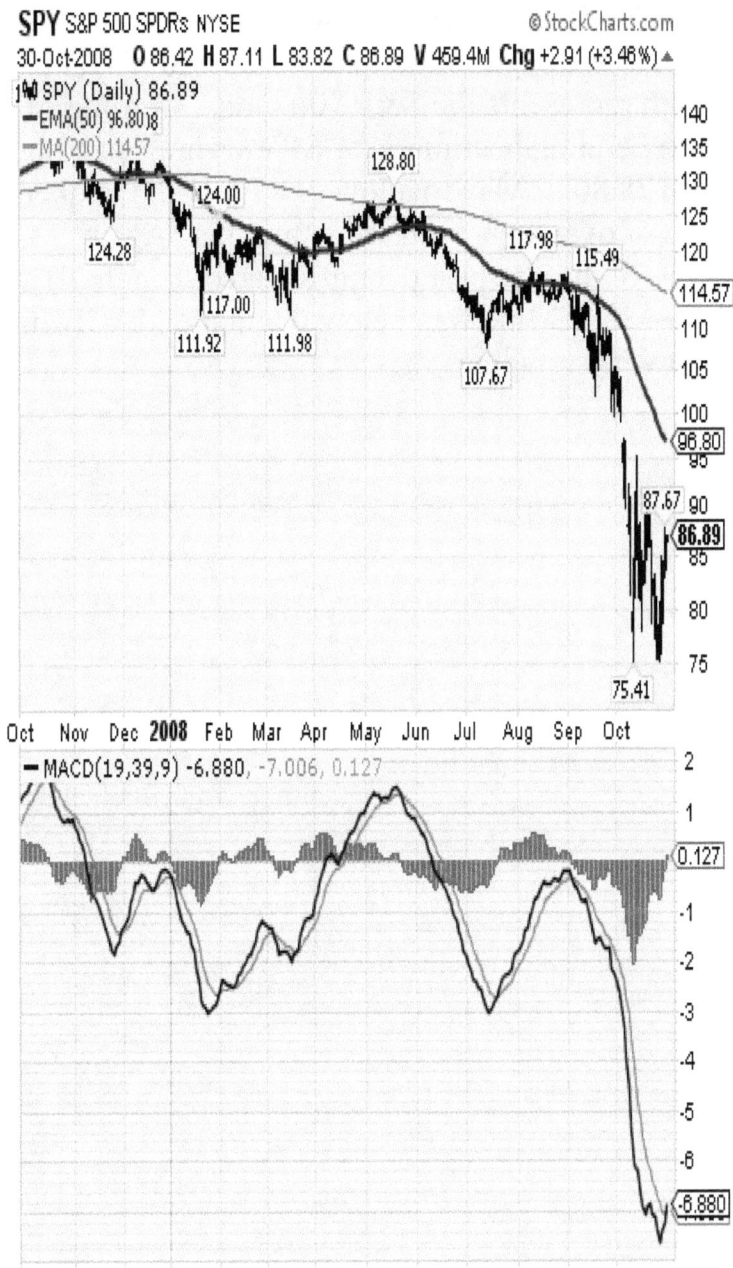

The 50 day EMA crossed below the 200 day SMA at the beginning of 2008 in the SPY ETF, which represents the S&P 500 index, warning of an impending bear market. SPY went from a high of $128.80 in May to a low of $75.41 in October, a drop of over 40% in just five months. Again, many of the sharpest declines were when the 19-39-9 MACD line was below 0 and the MACD line below its slow line.

GLD SPDR Gold Trust Shares NYSE
27-Aug-2013   **Close** 136.75 **Volume** 11.2M **Chg** +1.30 (+0.96%) ▲

W GLD (Daily) 136.75
—EMA(50) 129.84
—MA(200) 146.10

— MACD(19,39,9) 1.487, 0.671, 0.816

    In early December of 2012 the GLD ETF (Gold price) flashed a major sell signal when the GLD 19-39-9 MACD crossed below 0 with the MACD line below its slow line. In late February the 50 day EMA crossed below the 200 day SMA. From April 2013 through June 2013 GLD experienced a number of overnight and trading day downward gaps of 4% or more.

45

Chapter 7
Diversify

"You've got to look at the portfolio as a whole, not just position by position. And if you're trying to reduce the volatility or uncertainty of your portfolio as a whole, then you need more than one security obviously, but you also need securities which don't go up and down together."

-Harry Markowitz, Nobel Prize winner in economics

"Exchange-traded funds probably rank as the most successful financial product of the past two decades."

-Edward A. Finn Jr., Barron's October 19, 2009

It's important to diversify your portfolio and invest in a variety of financial markets. Much research indicates that a diversified portfolio reduces risks and draw downs. Investing in non-correlated markets help smooth the ups and downs of your portfolio value. Usually when some financial markets are going up, others are going down.

ETF's (Exchange traded funds) are a smart way to invest. You can invest in stocks, bonds, commodities, real estate, and currencies of the United States and many countries around the world. The difficulty with investing in individual stocks is that you are continually exposed to the risks of earnings announcements, CEO changes, takeovers, and other factors which can cause a stock to go down 10% or more overnight or during daytime trading hours.

An example of a well-diversified portfolio would be investing in a combination of the following ETF's:

VTI-Vanguard Total Stock Market U.S.

VEU-Vanguard FTSE All-World except U.S.

EWJ-Japan Stock Market I Shares

EEM-MSCI Emerging Stock Market I Shares

IWN-Russell 2000 Value I Shares (Small Cap Value Stocks)

VNQ-Vanguard Reits (Real Estate Stocks)

RWX-DJ Wilshire International Real Estate Stocks-Spdr's

GLD-Spdr Gold Trust Shares

DBC-DB Commodities Tracking Index

USO-United States Oil Fund, LP

HYG-I shares I Boxx High Yield Corporate Bonds

BND-Vanguard Total Bond

TLT- I Shares Barclays 20-year+ U.S. Treasury Bonds

BWX-Spdr Barclays Capital Intl Treasury Bond

EMB- I-shares JP Morgan USD Emerging Markets Bonds

UUP-Power Shares DB US Dollar Index Bullish

UDN-Power Shares DB US Dollar Index Bearish

There are hundreds of other ETF's that you could consider for your trading and investing. I especially like Vanguard ETF's due to their low expenses.

The important idea is that we want to buy ETF's which are trending up. It really doesn't make much difference whether we make our money by investing in an Italian stock index ETF, the Japanese currency, an emerging market bond index, a gold index, or a U.S. Stock market index. It is important to diversify your investments and get out of markets whose moving averages and momentum indicators are declining.

Chapter 8

A Simple, Profitable, Low Risk Trading System

"Knowledge is of no value, unless you put it into practice."

-Anton Chekhov

In summary, here is an example of an effective, profitable, and low risk trading system:

(1.)   First determine the overall trend of the market or ETF which you are trading. Make sure that the slope of the 50 day EMA is rising and the 50 day EMA is above the 200 day SMA.

(2.)   Using the 6-19-9 MACD or the 25-13-7 TSI (True Strength Index indicator, buy when the MACD or TSI line crosses above its slow line. You can also use the 14 day ADX for buy signals. When the +DMI crosses above the -DMI, a buy signal is given. As long as the overall trend is up, as defined in step 1 as listed above, you can also buy or re-enter a trade when an ADX trough is made confirmed by a few days of upward price action.

(3.)   Using the 19-39-9 MACD or the 15-9 TRIX (Triple Exponential Moving Average), sell when the MACD or TRIX line closes below its slow line. A sell signal is also given when the market is in an uptrend, an ADX peak is made confirmed by several days of downward price action.

(4.)   Stay out of all markets in which the 50 day EMA is below the 200 day SMA or when the 19-39-9 MACD line is below 0 and the MACD line is below its slow line. Diversify your investments and consider stocks, bonds, real estate (reits), commodities, and currency ETF's representing the United States and regions around the world.

After trading over 25 years in the financial markets and studying hundreds of books and trading systems, these are the best methods I have found to make money using stock charts. They are the methods I use to manage my own money.

Chapter 9
Mentally Speaking

"With self-discipline, most anything is possible."

-Theodore Roosevelt

"Have patience. All things are difficult before they become easy."

-Saadi

We have not discussed one of the most important factors in your trading success. Self-discipline and patience are two of the most important qualities you must develop to be successful in the financial markets. Sometimes you will go months without making money and have strings of losses. Other times you will record magnificent gains. Mentally you need to learn how to handle both.

You will be tempted to sell everything on big down days. When you are making big money, you may think the market has changed permanently and the good times will last forever.

You must absolutely learn to follow your trading plan and rules and not be swayed by a few big up or down days or weeks. You will never be successful if you are jumping in and out of the markets all the time on a whim or on emotions. Do not be switching from trading system to trading system. You *must* have *patience* and *self-discipline* to be successful. You will make most of your money when you are sitting and doing nothing. Remember that!

Chapter 10
Practice

"I play to win, whether during practice or a real game. And I will not let anything get in the way of me and my competitive enthusiasm to win."

-Michael Jordan

"I will prepare, and someday my chance will come."

-Abraham Lincoln

Now it's time to put theory into practice. The next ten pages will contain charts for you to make decisions. You need to get out some pencil and paper right now to do this practice.

Write down when you should have bought and sold on each chart and what your current position should be at the end of each chart. There will be an answer section at the end of the ten charts to see how well you did. Let's get started!

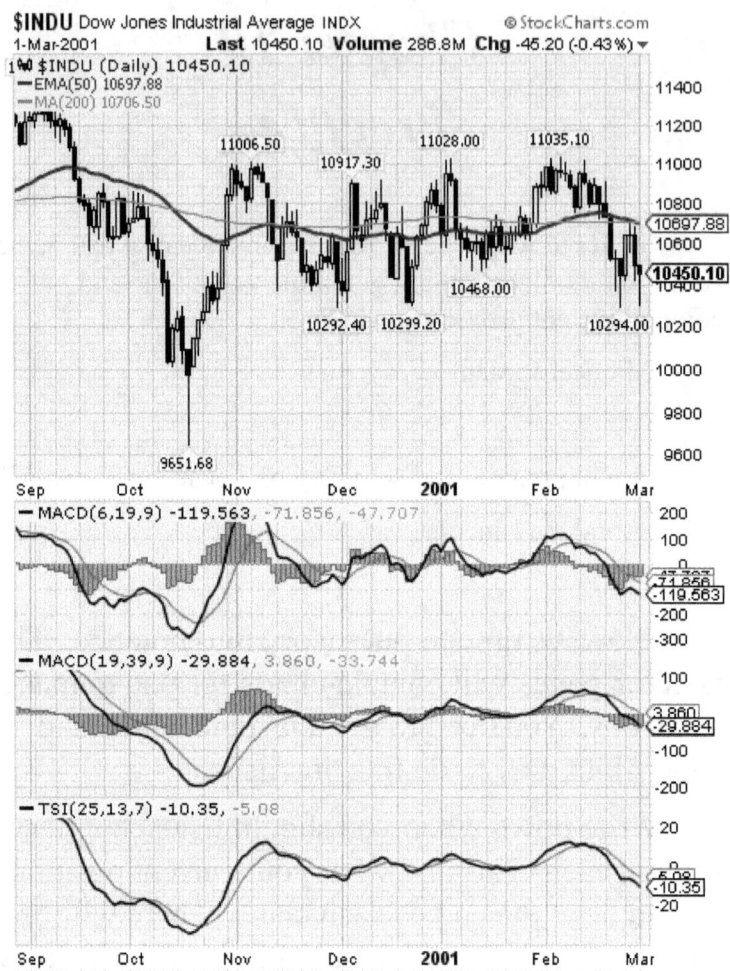

Chart 1 Dow Jones Industrial Average

Chart 2 Gold ETF

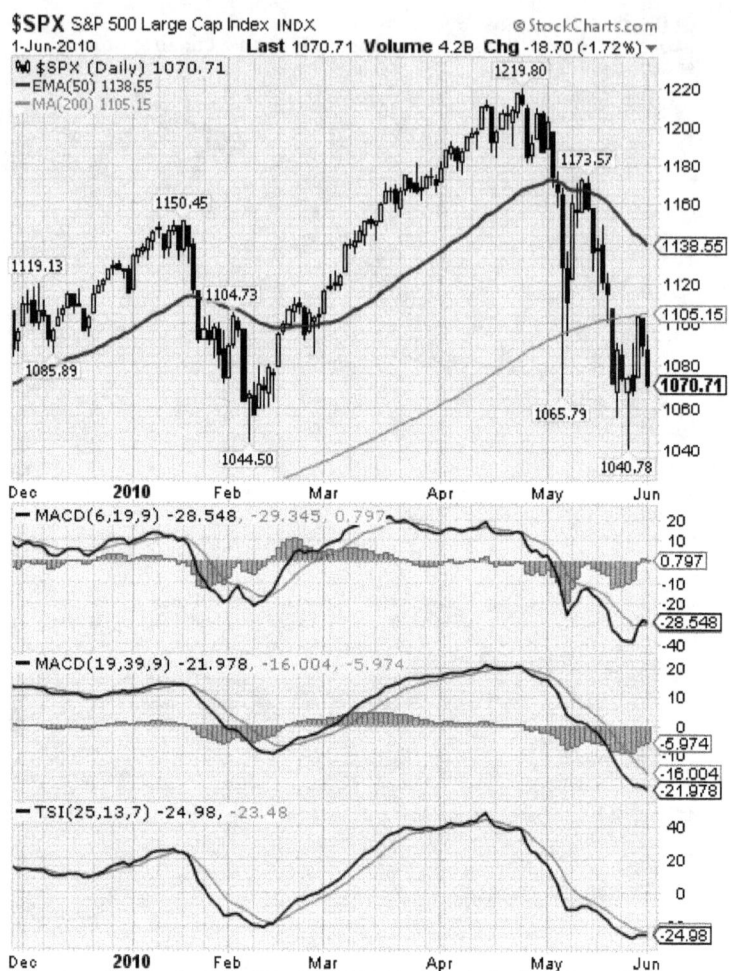

Chart 3 S&P 500 ETF

56

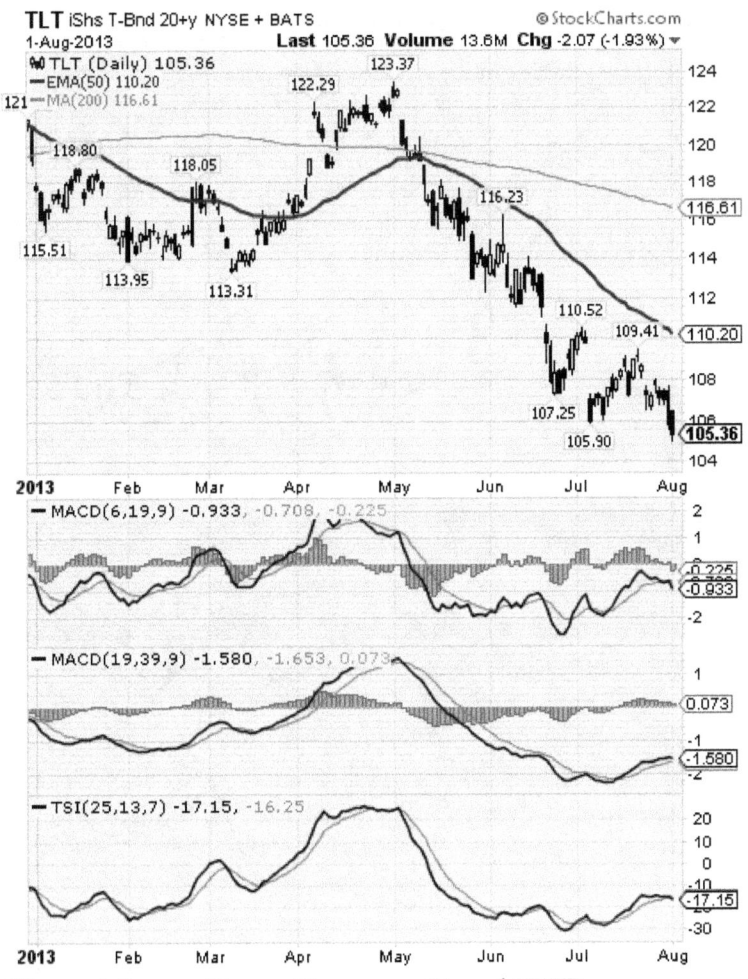

Chart 4 Long-Term Treasury Bond ETF

Chart 5 Japanese Currency FXY ETF

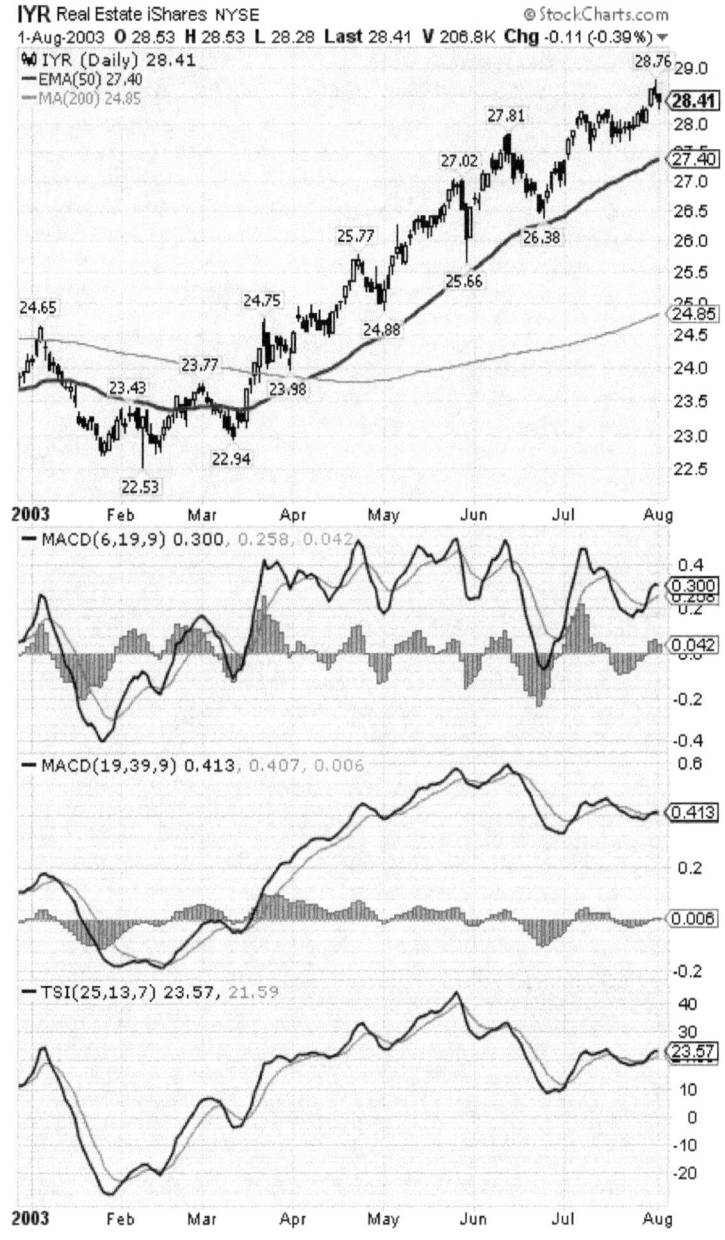

Chart 6 I Shares Real Estate ETF

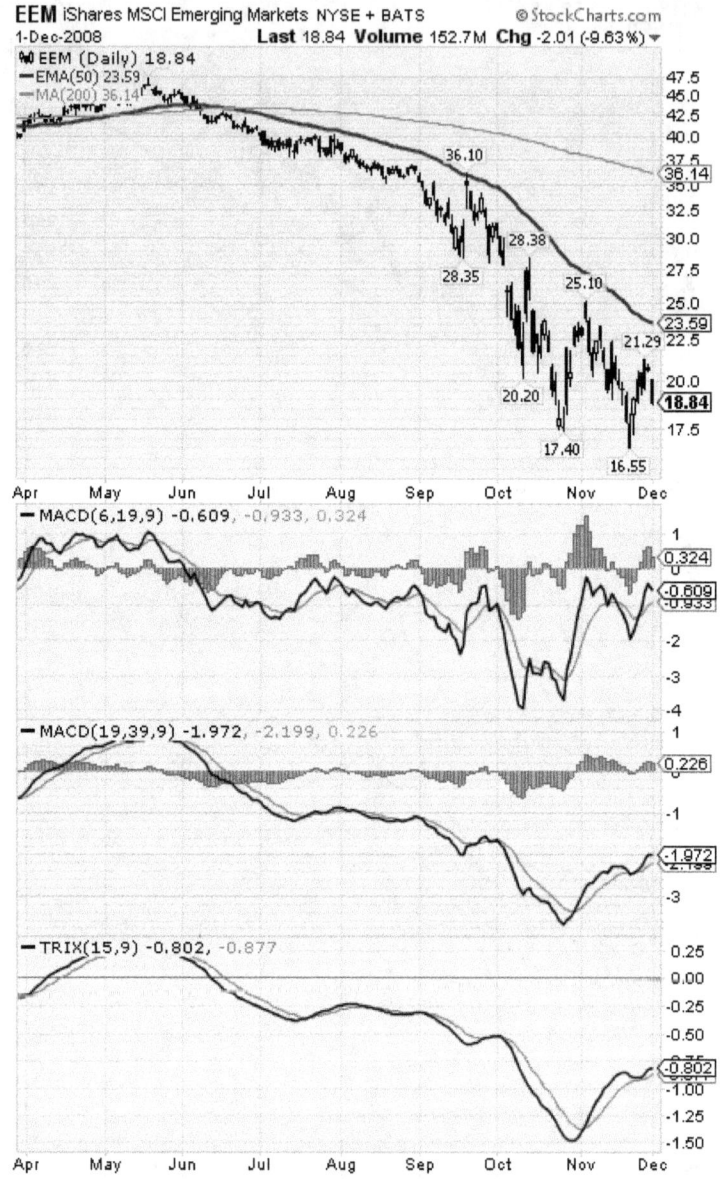

Chart 7 Emerging Stock Markets ETF

60

Chart 8 Japan Stock Market ETF

Chart 9 Bullish U.S. Dollar ETF   62

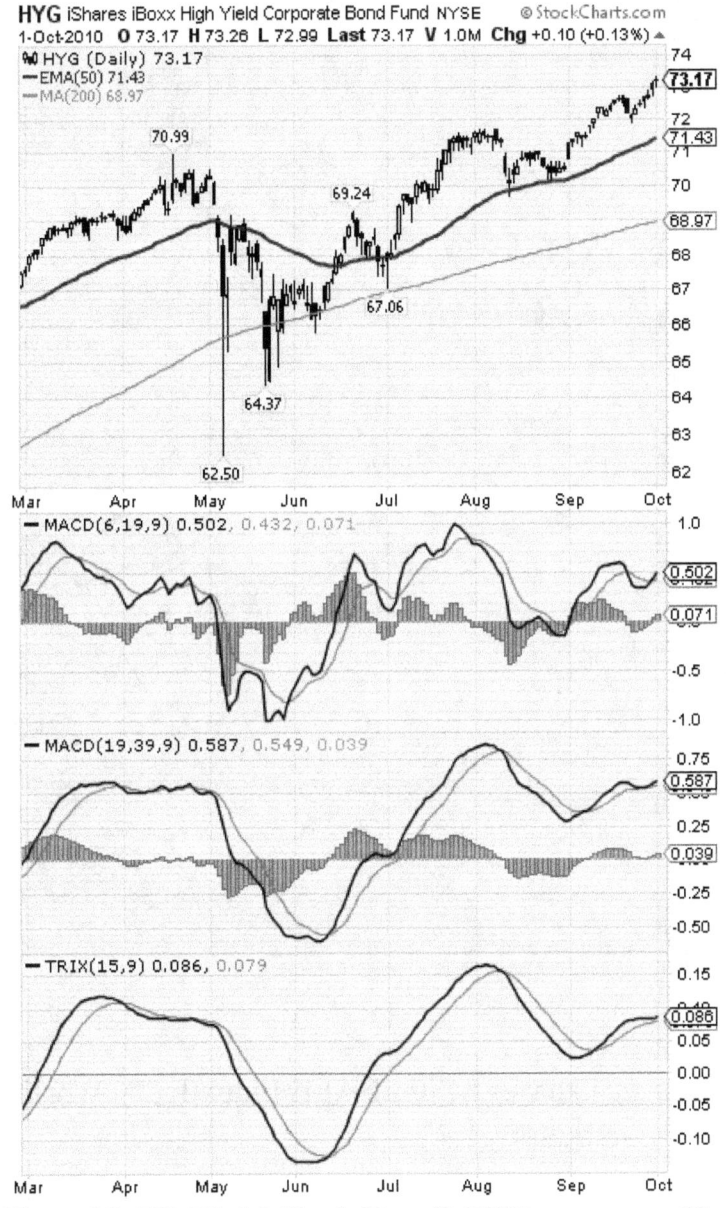

Chart 10 Hi-Yield (Junk Bond) ETF   63

Chart 11 I shares MSCI EAFE Index ETF (World
Stock Markets)

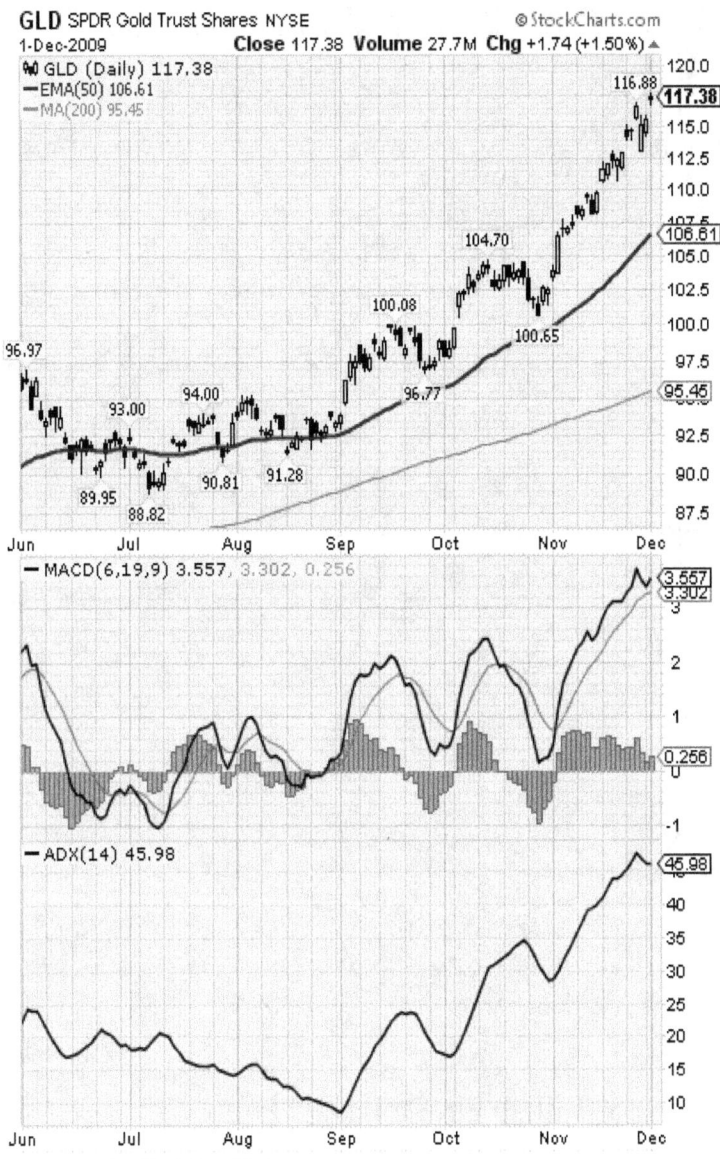

Chart 12 Gold ETF

Chart 13 Bullish US Dollar ETF

Practice Chart Answers

Chart 1- p.54- Although the 50 EMA is situated above the 200 SMA for much of this Dow Jones Industrial Average chart, the overall trend goes from down to sideways beginning in November of 2000. Moving averages are moving sideways. Stay away from trading this kind of chart, as it leads to whipsaws and many small losses.

Chart 2-p.55- The overall trend for the gold chart from the fall of 2005 to the spring of 2006 is up, as shown by the up trending 50 EMA above the up trending 200 SMA. A sell signal is given in early to mid-October by the 19-39-9 MACD lines and TSI line crossings. The market goes into a temporary sideways trend and then the 6-19-9 MACD and TSI line crossings issue timely buy signals in mid to late November. Notice how the 50 day EMA shows good support of price during the uptrend. At the right side of the chart another buy signal is indicated at the beginning of March by the 6-19-9 and TSI upward line crossings.

Chart 3-p.56- The trend is up at the beginning of this chart for the S&P 500 Index with the up sloping moving averages. In mid January 2010

19-39-9 MACD and TSI line crossings occur, along with a decreasing 50 day EMA. A sell signal is given at this point. In mid-February the 6-19-6 MACD and TSI line crossings signal a buy. Timely sell signals are given in mid-late April 2010 by the 19-39-9 MACD and TSI crossings, giving the trader advance notice to get out of the market before the steep decline which began in May. The investor would have been out of the market in plenty of time before the infamous "flash crash" which occurred in May of 2010.

Chart 4-p.57- This 2013 chart of TLT, the long term treasury bond ETF, indicates that the investor should have avoided this market. The 50 day EMA remained below the 200 day SMA for the entire time period. Although some buy signals were given during the time period by the 6-19-9 MACD and the TSI, the overall trend indicated by the placement of the moving averages remains down. In this case the MACD and TSI buy signals are ignored, because the overall trend of the market as shown by the moving averages is down. In these types of bear markets, any upward movements of price tend to be short-lived.

Chart 5-p.58- The Japanese Yen Currency ETF is in a severe bear market as show on this 2013 chart.

The 50 day EMA is good distance below the 200 day SMA, and both moving averages are moving sharply down. Despite some of the buy signals given by the 6-19-9 MACD and the 15-9 TRIX indicators, any rallies in price are short-lived. They are not worth buying because of the risk to the downside, as indicated by the sharply decreasing moving averages. The Japanese Yen was experiencing a great depression of its own.

Chart 6-p.59 – In this 2003 chart of the I shares real estate ETF IYR, timely buy signals are indicated in mid-March by the 6-19-6 MACD and TSI line crossings, in addition to the increasing 50 day EMA. In early April the 50 day EMA crosses above the 200 day SMA, confirming the upward trend. Again the increasing 50 day EMA provides solid support for prices during the uptrend. Although occasional sell signals are given by the 19-39-9 MACD and TSI crossings, re-entry signals are given by the 6-19-6 MACD crossovers. With a strongly up trending 50 day EMA as shown in this chart, sometimes it pays to wait a few days before before selling decisions are made using 19-39-9 MACD and TSI.

Chart 7-p.60 – The 19-39-9 MACD and TRIX flashed sell signals in late May to early June on this chart of EEM, the I shares Emerging Markets

ETF. With these indicators sloping sharply downward, the trader should have been out of this market much way before the 50 day EMA crossed downward through the 200 day SMA in late June. This chart shows the infamous crash of the equity markets of 2008. In mid-June the 19-39-9 MACD line is below 0 and is below its slow line, warning of the possibility of sharp declines or a possible market crash. The trader needs to take all such signals seriously and exit any market when the MACD line is below 0 and below its slow line. Although such setups do not always lead to sharp declines, they often do and are the conditions which occur before market crashes. In the space of about 6 months, EEM went from a price near $47 to a low of $16.55, a decline of over 60%. Using a few moving averages and MACD, the astute trader would have dodged one of the worst declines in stock market history.

Chart 8-p.61 – The 2007 chart of the Japan stock market index ETF EWJ shows a sideways market from April through July of 2007. The 50 day EMA is moving slightly down, sideways, and then slightly up, but can't seem to make up its mind as to its direction. This is the type of market which leads to many whipsaws and small losses. The trader needs to attempt to avoid trading in sideways markets. Finally in late July the 19-39-9 MACD and the TSI lines sharply cross their slower moving lines downward and the 50 day EMA begins a quick descent. The astute trader takes these signals as a definite sign to avoid this market. Although a nice rally attempt is made in September, the trader should avoid buying it. In September the 50 day EMA is still a good distance below the 200 day SMA, and the odds are high that any rally will be short-lived.

Chart 9-p. 62- The bullish dollar UUP ETF is finishing a nice uptrend at the beginning of this chart. In March of 2009 the 19-39-9 MACD and TSI experience sharp crossovers of their lines to the downside, indicating trouble ahead. Shortly thereafter, the 50 day EMA begins to decline. It is time to leave the market as soon as the MACD and TSI flash their warnings. The 50 day EMA crosses below the 200 day SMA in May, but the astute investor using the MACD and TSI are out of UUP in March, well ahead of the steep decline later in the year. Although the 6-19-6 MACD flashes a buy signal in very late March, it is best avoided due to the overall larger trend of the market. The buy signal is ignored because of the declining 50 day EMA. As a general rule, it is wise to avoid buying markets with *declining* 50 day EMA's, even the 50 day EMA is still situated above the 200 day SMA. The declining 50 day EMA served as ceiling to prices from May through December of 2009.

Chart 10-p. 63- The High Yield Corporate Bond ETF HYG is in an uptrend at the beginning of 2010. The first sign of trouble occurs in early April when price momentum begins to slow, as shown by the sideways trending MACD lines and the actual downward crossing of the TRIX line over its slow line. It is often a good time to lock in gains and avoid the market if momentum begins to slow, as it indicates a possible new downtrend developing. HYG experiences a sharp downtrend beginning in May, proving that the MACD and TRIX indicator warnings should have been heeded. In early June the 50 day EMA begins to rise again, and TRIX crosses its slow line at the time, indicating a buy point. At that point HYG continues a nice rise into October. Although a sell signal is given by 19-39-9 MACD and TRIX in early August, the up trending 50 day EMA continues to provide good support for prices through September. If the trader sells in early August, a good re-entry buy point into HYG is indicated by the 6-19-9 MACD line crossover at the beginning of September.

Chart 11-p.64 – The world stock markets ETF EFA is in uptrend during 2013. Timely exit points are given at the ADX peaks at the beginning of February, late May, and mid-August. These exit points match up perfectly with the 19-39-9 MACD and TRIX line crossings. Good re-entry buys are indicated by the ADX troughs in late March and early July, which are confirmed by several days of up price action.

Chart 12-p.65- The Gold ETF is trending sideways from June through August 2009. This is a market to avoid during that time, as we don't make money during sideways markets. The sideways trending is indicated by the flat 50 day EMA and the declining ADX. A major buying point occurs at the beginning of September with an ADX trough with a confirmation follow through of several days of rising prices, a crossing of the 6-19-9 MACD crossing above its slow line, and prices going strongly above the rising 50 day EMA, which is located above the 200 day SMA. Prices continue to rise sharply for the remainder of the year.

Chart 13-p.66- The Bullish U.S. Dollar ETF is in a definite downtrend for the last half of 2009. This is a market to avoid with down sloping moving averages and a MACD below 0 and below its slow line. This is a severe bear market that is subject to crashes and large amounts of capital loss if you were invested in this ETF. Ignore all the MACD buy signals and ADX peaks and troughs in this situation. The down sloping moving averages show that the overall trend is severely down.

Chapter 11
Questions and Answers

Q: In your examples you used ETF's and market indexes. Can I apply these methods to individual stocks and mutual funds?

A: Yes, these methods would also work well with individual stocks and mutual funds.

Q: Why do you often use different strategies or indicator settings on your exits as opposed to your entries?

A: Some indicator settings or methods work better for exits than entries, and vice-versa.

Q: How can I make money in a down market?

A: You can buy inverse ETF's or short individual stocks to make money in down markets. I have found it is more difficult to make money in bear markets because of the increase in volatility. Bear markets are simply more volatile than bull markets. Proshares are one of the largest sponsors of inverse ETF's in the world.

Q: I am new to reading stock charts, and these strategies are too complex for me. I am trying to do some market timing with my retirement accounts. What do you recommend for me?

A: *You could just choose a timing strategy from Chapter 3, which analyzes the overall trend. That would be superior to buying and holding. You will reduce your risk and avoid the large decreases in your equity value that accompany bear markets. And yes, bear markets are more common than you might think, and you will see many of them in your lifetime.*

Q: I like more complex trading methods and like to put many indicators on my charts for confirmations. What do you think?

A: *Several indicators on charts are all you need to be successful and reduce risks. If you overload your charts with numerous indicators, you will find it more difficult to make trading decisions. Many indicators will only confuse you and make charts more difficult to analyze.*

Q: Why do you use stock charts and indicators rather than studying the fundamentals of the stocks or the market such as earnings, news events, book values, price-earnings ratios, etc?

A: I personally have found that studying the "fundamentals" of the market to be complex, and sometimes obtaining accurate information can be difficult. I believe it is easier and more productive to read stock charts. A company can be very strong and have wonderful fundamentals, but many times those factors have little to do with future stock prices. A great company sometimes is a terrible stock to own, because its strength is not always reflected in its stock price. In other words a great company can have a lousy stock chart.

Q: What are other good methods of making money in the stock market besides reading stock charts?

A: Momentum and relative strength methods are also excellent strategies to make money in the market. An enormous amount of research in markets all over the world has shown that the strongest markets are the best places to invest. Strength tends to lead to more strength. For instance, the strongest stocks and markets over the last six months continue to have the highest probabilities of being the best stocks and markets in the coming months. It is the principle of inertia.

Q: What personal qualities must an investor have in order to make money in the markets?

A: Once a trader or investor has a good strategy or method, she must have a good self-discipline. She cannot be jumping out of the market on the first big down day, but must maintain the discipline of following her proven trading strategy.

A good trader has patience. Wait for the time when her strategy says to buy, and sell when it says to sell. Sometimes she will simply not be in the market. Warren Buffet, one of the greatest investors of all time, said that he makes most of his money when he is just sitting and doing nothing.

A good investor controls risks. He does not buy markets or stocks that are in big downtrends. Simply do not buy stocks or markets which are below their 200 day moving averages!

Q: There are many different kinds of moving averages. Which kind should I use?

A: It does not matter whether you use a simple, exponential, weighted, or any other particular kind of moving average on your charts. I use simple and exponential averages, because they are the most popular and are found in most charting programs. They all give about the same results.

Q: Can I expect a high percentage of my trades to be winners using the system described in this book?

A: Without doubt you will have some losing trades and occasionally experience some whipsaws. However, this system will you get you into trades which are big winners for much of the ride upward and will help you avoid bear markets. No system exists that is 100% accurate and successful in all its trades. On average you will make more money on your winning trades than what you lose on your losing trades. You may experience a string of losing trades in any good trading system, but in the long run what you make on your big winning trades should cancel out what you lose in a series of small losses.

Chapter 12
Recommended Resources

In order to implement these strategies, you will need a source to obtain good stock charts. You can obtain good charts many places on the web including:

Stockcharts.Com – The charts in this book are from Stockcharts.Com, and it is one of the most popular charting sites on the web.

Freecharts.Com – excellent charts

Good stock charts are often provided by your stockbroker, as part of their trading platform.

Some reliable, good discount brokers are Ameritrade, Interactive Brokers, Fidelity, Charles Schwab, Trade King, and Scottrade.

Amibroker is an excellent, inexpensive stand-alone charting program for do-it yourself investors.

A good book to read about another simple, but very effective investing strategy to time the financial markets is The Ivy Portfolio by Mebane T. Faber. His strategy uses a a monthly simple moving average to time buys and sells. His method has been back tested in many markets over many years and has been found to slightly increase profits and to greatly reduce risks and draw downs.

You can contact the author of this book with questions at: jogginguy@gmail.com

About the Author

George Kariger is a retired teacher from Argos Elementary School in Argos, Indiana. He is also the author of the book, <u>Our Kariger Family.</u> He has been a trader and investor in financial markets since 1985 and has spent thousands of hours intensely studying numerous market trading books, articles, research, and systems. He regularly had his students participate in stock market simulation contests when he was a teacher. In 2001 one of his fifth grade teams defeated over 2000 other stock market teams in Indiana to win the state contest. His team made over $36,000 in only ten weeks on an investment of $100,000 in the spring of 2001. This amazing feat was accomplished during a severe down stock market. He had numerous other teams over his many years of teaching who finished in the top ten in state stock market simulations.

He has a B.S. Degree from Manchester College and a M.S. Degree from the University of St. Francis. George lives in Fort Wayne, Indiana.

Notes

Notes